# A Crazy, Holy Grace
# Participant Guide

# A CRAZY, HOLY GRACE
## THE HEALING POWER OF PAIN AND MEMORY

### *A Crazy, Holy Grace: Participant Guide*

978-1-5018-5831-4
978-1-5018-5832-1 eBook

### *A Crazy, Holy Grace: Leader Guide*

978-1-5018-5833-8
978-1-5018-5834-5 eBook

### *A Crazy, Holy Grace: DVD*

978-1-5018-5835-2

### *A Crazy, Holy Grace*
### *The Healing Power of Pain and Memory*

978-0-310-34976-1
978-0-310-35054-5 eBook

PARTICIPANT GUIDE

# A CRAZY, HOLY GRACE

The Healing Power *of* Pain and Memory.

## FREDERICK BUECHNER

Participant Guide
by Michael S. Poteet

Abingdon Press / Nashville

# A Crazy, Holy Grace:
## The Healing Power of Pain and Memory
## Participant Guide

978-1-5018-5831-4

18 19 20 21 22 23 24 25 26 27 — 10 9 8 7 6 5 4 3 2 1
MANUFACTURED IN THE UNITED STATES OF AMERICA

# Contents

# Contents

# Introduction

For more than six decades, novelist and Presbyterian minister Frederick Buechner has been one of the world's most popular and eloquent interpreters of the Bible and Christian faith. *A Crazy, Holy Grace* combines rich excerpts from several of his earlier works with a new essay, "The Gates of Pain," to offer an extended, autobiographical meditation on the nature of suffering and how Christians can both survive their pain and move beyond it into a joyful vision of hope.

In Chapter 1, "The Gates of Pain," Buechner contrasts the familiar ways we handle our pain with being "good stewards" of it instead. He explores what good stewardship of pain looks like with a fresh reading of Jesus' Parable of the Talents. In Chapter 2, "A Crazy, Holy Grace," Buechner recalls the childhood years he spent in Bermuda as an example of how we can look back at our lives for God's unexpected, gracious gifts. Finding evidence of God's goodness in the past can bolster our faith in God's goodness now. In the third chapter, "A Room Called Remember," Buechner encourages readers to think of remembering as a spiritual discipline. Taking King David in 1 Chronicles 16 as his biblical example, Buechner discusses the way our memories can reveal God's ongoing work in our lives.

Chapter 4, "The Magic of Memory," invites readers to listen in on an imagined but prayerful conversation Buechner has with his dead grandmother. To remember, Buechner suggests, is to practice powerful magic that can connect us with those in our lives and, perhaps, give us greater insight into what awaits us after death. In Chapter 5, "The Struggle of Memory," Buechner reflects on his relationship with his dead brother, Jamie. Their relationship reveals clues about what it means to live an authentic life, and Buechner learns what it means, as the letter to the Ephesians says, to see with "the eyes of your heart."

In Chapter 6, "The Hope of Memory," Buechner evaluates the witness he has borne in his life to Christian hope, and he tells readers what he really believes about the hope to which God calls us. Emotional pain and strong memory are two of the most powerful experiences human beings can know. Buechner's book illuminates multiple connections between the two and suggests ways that God uses them both to heal and to hallow us.

I was once fortunate enough to hear Frederick Buechner preach. As I shook his hand on my way out the door after worship, I told him how much his written words had meant to me over the years. He looked at me with an apparently utterly authentic look of surprise on his face, and asked, gently and sincerely, "Really?" His response rang no note of false humility. I am confident that many, many people have told him the same over his career. But in that moment, he seemed genuinely surprised and grateful that his words could have had such an impact on anyone, let alone an impact for the good.

This book is intended as a companion volume to *A Crazy, Holy Grace: The Healing Power of Pain and Memory* by Frederick Buechner (Zondervan, 2017). Readers can use it on their own, or as part of a group study, and they will get the most out of this guide by reading it alongside Buechner's book. Each section begins with a summary of the corresponding section or sections of *A Crazy, Holy Grace.*

After each summary, this guide presents studies of biblical passages either quoted by Buechner or suggested by his subjects and themes, followed by questions for personal reflection. These sections are intended not only to increase readers' appreciation of the ways Buechner interacts with and interprets Scripture and the Christian tradition, but also to provide a basis for readers' own, biblically informed reflections on the issues Buechner's book raises.

The "Personal Response" sections offer generally shorter reflections on a third passage of Scripture, intended to help readers apply Scripture, as well as Buechner's insights, to their own lives. Finally, each section concludes with a devotional and a prayer, offered in the hope that this guide can be a useful aid to personal worship. It is my hope that this guide moves readers to engage directly with Buechner's work and, even more importantly, to relate more deeply to the God who transforms pain and memory into blessing and new life.

Session 1

# The Gates of Pain

The Gates of Pain

# Session 1

# The Gates of Pain

### SUMMARY

*The Universality of Pain*

Frederick Buechner remembers a night when he was a boy when his mother told him to keep his father's car keys away from him because he had been drinking. His father came into Buechner's bedroom and asked for the keys, but Buechner said nothing. He clutched the keys in his fist under his pillow and kept the bedcovers over his head until his father fell asleep. It is one of Buechner's early experiences and memories of pain.

Buechner acknowledges pain's universality: "No matter who you are, how lucky or unlucky, or rich or poor, or this or that, part of what it means to be a human being in this world is to labor and be heavy laden, to be in need of whatever [Jesus] means by rest."

He discusses four principal ways people attempt to cope with pain, although he allows that there are many others, most or all of which most of us have tried, at some time and to some degree:

1. **We can try to forget our pain.** Buechner says this is how his mother dealt with the pain of his father's suicide (when Buechner was ten years old) and two unsuccessful marriages. This option of dealing with pain costs us the chance to grow as compassionate human beings. We fail to open ourselves to the reality that we are not the only people who feel pain.

2. **We become trapped in our pain.** Buechner illustrates this survival method by discussing two of Charles Dickens's characters—Miss Havisham in *Great Expectations* and Mrs. Gummidge in *David Copperfield*—who allow their pain to define and confine them.

3. **We make light of our pain.** Buechner remembers a friend's daughter who told him how terrible her marriage was but who laughed about it, as though it were a joke.

4. **We compete with other people's pain.** In this survival method, pain "becomes a kind of accomplishment." "You think you've had it bad?" we ask others. "Let me tell you what's happened to me!"

## Good Stewardship of Pain

In contrast to these ways of coping with pain, Buechner suggests living as a "good steward" of our pain. He explains what he means by discussing Jesus' Parable of the Talents (Matthew 25:14-30 NRSV).

In Buechner's reading of this parable, the talents the master gives his servants represent "whatever it is that life deals us," including our experiences of suffering and pain. The servant who buries his talent out of fear angers his master because the master expected him to do something productive with what he'd been given. Similarly, God "expects that out of whatever the world in its madness does to us, we will somehow reap a harvest."

Buechner stresses he does not believe that God causes pain, but that God does expect us to find treasure in it, treasure that we can then share with others. The single-talent servant's fate at the parable's end is not so much a punishment as a consequence of his failure to be a good steward of his pain: "If you bury your life—if you don't face, among other things, your pain—your life shrinks. . . . It is in a way taken away." When we "bury whatever it is that the world gives [us], and then live as carefully as [we] can without really living at all," we "have less life every day." Buechner compares the third servant's situation to a cricket he found trapped in his room: "To live closed up in yourself, as that cricket was closed up in the room, is itself wailing and gnashing of teeth."

The other two servants, by contrast, "traded" with their pain. They gave of themselves to others by honestly living out of their pain. Buechner experienced the power of such "life-traders" for himself when his friends went out of their way to visit him while his eldest daughter was sick in a hospital, almost dying of anorexia. "They offered no suffocating good advice," he recalls, "or platitudinous explanations of why bad things happen to reasonably good people. They were just there." Buechner also points to twelve-step groups as places where people are present with each other in the midst of pain—and, as a result, open themselves to new possibilities of healing and life.

### "Pain Is Treasure"

Buechner asks why God often seems distant and silent during times of suffering. He decides the silence is actually God's "passionate restraint"—"As I dream him, he wants so much to be able to step in and make things right, but how can God do that without destroying what life is all about?" Instead, Buechner suspects God sends people like his friends to be "life-givers, life-savers" who are willing to be present with others in pain and to share that pain with them.

Buechner says our pain is the most precious thing we human beings can give each other. Why? When we relate to each other out of our pain, we relate to each other as who we really are. Buechner wishes he had been able to relate to his father that way on the night he kept the car keys. He wonders how his and his father's lives might have been different if they had been able to admit their fear to each other that night in Buechner's room.

And when we speak out of our personal depths, we find ourselves and each other, and even God, in those depths. When we speak with each other out of our pain, that pain can become the gateway to the ultimate joy God has promised.

## SCRIPTURE REFLECTION

1. **Matthew 25:14-30**

   *"The kingdom of heaven is like a man who was leaving on a trip. He called his servants and handed his possessions over to them. To one he gave five valuable coins, and to another he gave two, and to another he gave one. He gave to each servant according to that servant's ability. Then he left on his journey.*

   *"After the man left, the servant who had five valuable coins took them and went to work doing business with them. He gained five more. In the same way, the one who had two valuable coins gained two more. But the servant who had received*

the one valuable coin dug a hole in the ground and buried his master's money.

"Now after a long time the master of those servants returned and settled accounts with them. The one who had received five valuable coins came forward with five additional coins. He said, 'Master, you gave me five valuable coins. Look, I've gained five more.'

"His master replied, 'Excellent! You are a good and faithful servant! You've been faithful over a little. I'll put you in charge of much. Come, celebrate with me.'

"The second servant also came forward and said, 'Master, you gave me two valuable coins. Look, I've gained two more.'

"His master replied, 'Well done! You are a good and faithful servant. You've been faithful over a little. I'll put you in charge of much. Come, celebrate with me.'

"Now the one who had received one valuable coin came and said, 'Master, I knew that you are a hard man. You harvest grain where you haven't sown. You gather crops where you haven't spread seed. So I was afraid. And I hid my valuable coin in the ground. Here, you have what's yours.'

"His master replied, 'You evil and lazy servant! You knew that I harvest grain where I haven't sown and that I gather crops where I haven't spread seed? In that case, you should have turned my money over to the bankers so that when I returned, you could give me what belonged to me with interest. Therefore, take from him the valuable coin and give it to the one who has ten coins. Those who have much will receive more, and they will have more than they need. But as for those who don't have much, even the little bit

*they have will be taken away from them. Now take
the worthless servant and throw him outside into the
darkness.'*

*"People there will be weeping and grinding their
teeth."*

If you've ever worked a job in which you were responsible for accomplishing an important task or producing significant results in your boss's absence, you may be able to relate to the three servants in what's popularly known as Jesus' "Parable of the Talents" (in the Bible, parables have no formal titles unless modern editors put them there). As Buechner recognizes in his imaginative reading of this parable, its main interest is not the talents themselves but what the servants do or fail to do with them.

In the first century, a day laborer would have to work fifteen years to earn one talent.[1] To call this amount a "valuable coin," as the Common English Bible (CEB) does, hardly does it justice. The master in the story entrusts his servants with enormous sums— even though he himself characterizes them as "little" (25: 21, 23).

Each of the first two servants doubles the amount his master gives them. The story doesn't say specifically how. The assumption that they "traded with them" (25:16 NRSV) seems reasonable. "Because most people did not have capital available for investment," notes biblical scholar Craig S. Keener, "those who did could reap large profits," as do these servants.[2]

But we shouldn't let twenty-first-century experiences of investment trading color our ideas about their activity too much. The Greek verb in Matthew 25:16 is *ērgasato*,[3] derived from *ērgo*, "to work." (You might recognize in that word the origin of the "erg" as a scientific unit of work.)[4] The CEB captures the sense more directly: These servants "went to work doing business" with their talents.

If they traded, they were not far removed from the transactions as modern traders are, buying and selling complicated financial products online at lightning speed. These servants were *working*—putting forth effort, shouldering risk, getting involved in hands-on ways.

For his part, the master, upon his return, doesn't ask *how* the first two servants grew the money. He only praises them for having done it, before rewarding them by giving them more and calling them to celebrate with him. But he condemns the third servant for having done *nothing* with the money—for not even putting it in the ancient equivalent of a minimum interest-bearing savings account!

The third servant was afraid because he thought of his master as "a hard man" (25:24)—that is, a strong and harsh man, a difficult man. And the master confirms the servant's opinion of him, in both word (25:26) and action (25:30).

But he is not so harsh as to reject one servant because he did not produce the same ROI (return on investment) as another. The master says he would have accepted some return, *any* return, from his investment in the third servant (25:27). In this respect, we might even think the master generous! After all, not too many employers would tell their employees during performance reviews, "You didn't make me as much money as so-and-so over there, but I'm thrilled you made me any money at all! Let's go have a drink." What the master cannot accept is, as Buechner says, the third servant's sloth—his decision to let fear keep him from *working*, as his fellow servants *worked*.

In Matthew, this parable serves as a lesson about how disciples should best use the time before Jesus comes at "the end of the age" (24:3). (Contrast Luke's version, 19:11-27, which highlights the difference between earthly kings and Jesus as king.)[5] It immediately precedes Jesus' parable about the last judgment, when the nations will be rewarded or condemned based on whether they fed the hungry, clothed the naked, welcomed the stranger, cared for the sick, visited the imprisoned—all examples of *work* that requires personal, hands-on involvement and investment (Matthew 25:31-46).

As Buechner reads it, this parable is not about what to do before Jesus comes, but about what to do in order to fully live. And he makes clear he knows that the kind of trading Jesus calls for is hard work. "I'm talking now," he writes, "about what it means to trade with your pain, as the good and faithful servants traded with their talents. . . . It's hard to share not just the shallows of your life, which is what we're all so good at doing, but to speak out of the depths of your life—the depths are scary." But when we do that hard work, says Buechner, we find ourselves, each other, and Christ.

*Questions for Reflection*
- In which way of surviving pain that Buechner identifies do you most recognize yourself, and why?
- Do you agree with Buechner that being good stewards of our pain is "a marvelous idea?" Why or why not?
- Why does Buechner call Jesus' Parable of the Talents "a dark and frightening and fascinating story?" Do you agree? Why or why not?
- When was a time you let fear keep you from working and taking risks with your "talent?" When was a time that you did the work and took the risks? What happened in each case?
- Buechner writes that God's forgiveness, compassion, and mercy mean "you dare take your chances and do what you can with the hand that life, or God, has dealt you."

How does your view of God's character motivate you to make the choices you make in life?

- Buechner says God is present in our life's depths, as well as in our life's heights. How do you experience God's presence in your own and others' times of suffering and times of joy?

2. **Job 2:11-13**

> When Job's three friends heard about all this disaster that had happened to him, they came, each one from his home—Eliphaz from Teman, Bildad from Shuah, and Zophar from Naamah. They agreed to come so they could console and comfort him. When they looked up from a distance and didn't recognize him, they wept loudly. Each one tore his garment and scattered dust above his head toward the sky. They sat with Job on the ground seven days and seven nights, not speaking a word to him, for they saw that he was in excruciating pain.

Buechner doesn't specifically cite the book of Job when writing about the life-traders who helped him survive the emotional and spiritual pain he suffered during his daughter's hospitalization. But his description of how his three friends ("Lou," Bill Welch, and Paul Beaman) supported and comforted him mirrors the biblical account of how Job's friends Eliphaz, Bildad, and Zophar support and comfort Job—at least initially—as Job sits on the ash heap of his possessions, scraping his sores with a pottery shard, mourning the deaths of his children.

Like Buechner's friends, Job's friends "trade" their lives. They give up their own for a time, "each one from his home" (2:11), in order to be with someone who is suffering. As Lou tells Buechner, "I knew it was a bad time for you; I just thought it might be nice to have somebody, an extra friend, around." Buechner's friends don't wail and tear their garments when they see him, as Job's do, but they are simply present with him in his pain as Job's friends were present with Job in his.

Their actions resemble the Jewish practice of "sitting *shiva*": surrounding people who are bereaved for seven days after the death with a community that will take care of their needs. Ron Wolfson, a professor at American Jewish University, writes that "the fundamental message of Judaism about death and bereavement" is, "We are not alone."[6] "The great genius of Jewish bereavement," Wolfson writes, "is to empower the community to be God's partner in comforting those who mourn."[7] Although Buechner isn't Jewish, he sees his life-trading friends as "sent by God" to comfort him: "not in the sense he moved them there, but something in the mysterious air of the world wafted them there, because that air, like the rest of the world, proceeds from the mouth of God."

The book of Job begins (chapters 1–2) and ends (42:7-17) in narrative prose. The conventional image of "the patience of Job" comes from these sections, as Job endures all his calamities with "absolute integrity" (2:3), refusing to curse the God from whose hands, he believes, come both good and evil (as he believes; the narrative reveals that God has allowed "the Adversary"—*ha satan* in Hebrew, from which "Satan" is derived—to make Job suffer).

But the majority of the book (3:1–42:6) is poetry. And in this poetry, Job does not sound so patient. He speaks out of his pain angrily and repeatedly, lamenting his losses, demanding he be allowed to argue for just treatment from God (among many examples are 10:1-3; 16:7-17; 23:1-5).

Job's friends also speak in the poetry, breaking their silence to offer exactly the "good advice" and "platitudinous explanations" of suffering that Buechner's friends avoided. Job's friends stop *sharing* Job's pain and instead attempt to explain it. They defend God's honor and justice (8:1-7), insisting that Job must have committed some sin worthy of such punishment (11:6-11), or that God is trying to teach Job a lesson for Job's own good (5:17-27). Job rejects these explanations, even though they echo much traditional thinking about suffering found in Hebrew Scripture. He calls his friends "miserable comforters" (16:2 NRSV).

And God agrees with him. While God doesn't give Job the answers he wants, neither does God endorse the answers Job's friends gave. Instead, God is "angry" at the friends "because [they] haven't spoken about me correctly as did my servant Job" (42:7). In the book as we have it, God's statement can only refer back to the friends' theologically orthodox explanations, contrasted with Job's own honest, anguished argument with God.

God appears to approve, then, of the stewardship of pain Buechner calls for: "You don't have to talk about pain, but you have to live out of your pain. Speak out of your depths. Speak out of who you truly are." We should engage in honest conversations, with God and with others, that come out of our pain.

And when we are moved to comfort others, we should follow the *first* example Job's friends set, and the example Buechner's friends set: simply and silently being present. That can be, as it was for Buechner, "a blessed event, a holy event." In such silence, as we give space for those who suffer to say whatever they will, we "speak" more correctly about God, who gives us all space and grace to feel what we really feel and to be who we really are.

*Questions for Reflection*

- What's the worst thing someone has said to you when you were suffering?
- What's the worst thing you've said to someone else who was suffering?
- Who have been "life-traders" for you—people who have simply and silently been present with you in your pain?
- Buechner rejects the idea that God causes us pain: "God doesn't deal with the world that way; he doesn't move us around like chess pieces." What do you believe about God's relationship to our pain and suffering?
- When we suffer, Buechner suggests, God cannot "step in and make things right ... without destroying what life is all about," because then we would not be free. What do you think of this idea? Can and does God intervene when we suffer without compromising who we are as human beings? Why or why not?
- Buechner quotes Jesus' cry from the cross: "My God, my God, why have you left me?" (Matthew 27:46; Mark 15:34) What is the significance of Jesus' cry? How, if at all, does it shape the way you relate to God when you are in pain?

## PERSONAL RESPONSE

Buechner describes how, during his daughter's illness, Psalm 131 became exactly the psalm he needed to read. He calls it his "magic talisman" because he came across it by opening his Bible at random, and could not, in that moment, recall ever having read it before:

> LORD, *my heart isn't proud;*
> *my eyes aren't conceited.*
> *I don't get involved with things too great or*
> *wonderful for me.*
> No. *But I have calmed and quieted myself*
> *like a weaned child on its mother;*
> *I'm like the weaned child that is with me.*
>
> *Israel, wait for the* LORD—
> *from now until forever from now!*
> *Psalm 131*

Psalm 131 is one of the "songs of ascents" (Psalms 120–134), the psalms pilgrims in ancient Israel likely sang as they traveled up to Jerusalem to worship at the Temple.[8] This brief psalm's final verse echoes Psalm 130's emphasis on waiting for God and may have originally been read together with that psalm.

As the CEB's translation indicates, the psalm-singer might have been a woman and mother, carrying her "weaned child" with her. Certainly, as Buechner notes, the psalm is also notable for presenting a female, maternal image for God. The Bible does contain other explicitly maternal and feminine images for God (for example, Isaiah 42:14; 66:13; Matthew 23:37 and Luke 13:34), but they are not as prevalent as paternal and masculine ones, so such images can play a special role in expanding and enriching our view of God.

Buechner says God helped him through Psalm 131 because the psalm spoke directly to his emotional situation: "My eyes were not lifted up, my heart was not high. I was not occupying myself with anything except how I was going to survive the sight of my child." When we are standing at the beginning of what we know will be a long and difficult journey out of the depths—a physical climb up from a low place to a higher one, as the ancient worshipers faced, or an emotional and spiritual climb up from deep suffering and pain, as Buechner faced—we can find the strength for the road ahead by waiting on God, who nurses us like a loving mother until we are satisfied with peace—what the apostle Paul called "the peace of God, which transcends all understanding," that "guard[s] [our] hearts and your minds in Christ Jesus" (Philippians 4:7 NRSV).

- Have you, like Buechner, ever experienced reading a passage of Scripture in so fresh and powerful a way that it seems like you have never really read that passage before? If so, which passage? How did the experience affect you?
- Why does Buechner call Psalm 131 his "magic talisman?" Do you have or have you had a Scripture passage that has seemed almost magical to you? How?
- How do feminine and maternal images for God, like the one in Psalm 131, shape your understanding of and personal relationship with God?
- When have you faced a long and difficult "ascent" from the depths? Who and what helped you make the journey?
- How, specifically, do you "wait for the LORD," as Psalm 131 urges?

# DEVOTION

*"Come to me, all you who are struggling hard and carrying heavy loads, and I will give you rest. Put on my yoke, and learn from me. I'm gentle and humble. And you will find rest for yourselves. My yoke is easy to bear, and my burden is light."*

*Matthew 11:28-30*

*Throw all your anxiety onto him, because he cares about you.*

*1 Peter 5:7*

I wasn't there to see it for myself. But I recently heard about something that made me think about what Buechner is talking about when he talks about life-trading—about being truly present with others in the midst of their pain.

My son plays the flute in his school's band. For three out of the four quarters in every Friday night's football game, the band sits in the bleachers, ready to play bouncy and boisterous tunes at every touchdown or turnover in the home team's favor. But during the third quarter, the instruments are down, and the band has a chance to eat snacks and socialize.

During one recent third quarter, my son noticed the band's drum major sitting by himself, head buried in his hands, weeping. According to my son, the drum major is not (contrary to what I, at least, would have expected) a popular kid. He doesn't have many friends. And—again, if my son is to be believed, and I can only tell you that I think he is—the drum major does a fair amount to bring it on himself. I've heard several stories of how he's very self-centered and unappreciative of the band's best efforts, and really only views his drum major status as a bullet point on his college applications.

But this night, the drum major was alone and weeping. He wasn't hiding, said my son—he was simply isolated, and being actively ignored by the rest of the band as he wept. And my son told me later, "I thought, 'Look, so maybe he's not always the nicest guy, but are you just going to do *nothing* while he sits there crying?'"

And so my son went to go sit with him. And he heard from the drum major how band members he thought were his friends had been talking about him behind his back, mocking him, calling him some ugly and demeaning names. My son simply sat with him and listened, and put a hand on his back to try to comfort him. He said it felt really awkward, but that it also felt like the right thing to do.

If I were going to write a fictional short story about this incident, I'd be tempted to do the obvious thing and cast my son as the hero who helped the drum major see the error of his ways. In the next scene, they would be fast friends, and my son would be helping facilitate the mutual apologies that sound as though they are needed in the band, and his act of going to sit with the drum major as he sobbed in the stands would have been noticed and praised as a real turning point for everyone.

Of course, none of that happened. The other band members ignored my son and the drum major together, just as they ignored the drum major when he was alone. And my son says the drum major is still arrogant and mean-spirited. I suppose that is one way he is choosing to deal with his pain, which sounded real and raw to my son that night.

Maybe I'm just indulging proud parental instincts, or maybe I'm too quick to believe my son's account of the incident. But, assuming all happened as he said it did, my son took it upon himself to be a life-trader that night. He tried to do something that would help the drum major with his heavy load of pain, a heavy load that is different for all of us but which Jesus calls us all to bring to him (Matthew 11:28).

We gain immensely more than we give when we trade our life, our pain, with Jesus—when we cast our cares on him because he cares for us (1 Peter 5:7). The trade isn't equal. But it is true. He is willing to take all our pain upon himself in order that we might share all his joy, not just in the life to come, but starting here and now.

*Loving God, who experienced the depths of human pain in your Son's suffering and death: By your Spirit, give us courage to feel the pain of others so that together we may grow into the people you mean us to be, showing the world your power to heal and make new. Amen.*

Session 2

# A Crazy, Holy Grace

# Session 2

# A Crazy, Holy Grace

## SUMMARY

*Once-Upon-a-Time*

Frederick Buechner remembers the day his father killed himself. He was ten years old; his brother, Jamie, was almost eight. They woke up early that Saturday morning in the late autumn of 1936 and were playing with a roulette wheel when their father opened their bedroom door to look in on them. As Buechner presents it, the moment was completely unremarkable: "There was nothing to suggest that he opened the door for any reason other than just to check on us as he passed by on his way to the bathroom or wherever else we might have thought he was going that early on a Saturday morning, if either of us had bothered to think about it at all."

But the moments that followed were anything but ordinary. A shout shattered the house's stillness. Sent back to their room after the sudden commotion, the boys looked out a window and saw their father lying on his back in the driveway, Buechner's mother and grandmother were pumping his legs, trying in vain to revive him. A doctor arrived, also too late. Days later, the family found a suicide note.

Ever since that morning, Buechner has been keenly aware of his mortality. His father's suicide ended his "once-below-a-time"— by which he means a time of innocence and a (mistaken) sense of immortality—and began his "once-upon-a-time," in which he has been aware that, one day, his own end will come.

But Buechner did not grieve his father's death the way his brother did, and he thinks a large part of the reason why was because he, Jamie, and their mother moved soon after the suicide to Bermuda—a land so exotic and colorful it was, for Buechner, no less enchanted than the Land of Oz or Never Never Land.

### The Isle Gives Delight, and Hurts Not

Although Buechner's paternal grandmother paid for the move to Bermuda and rented the family's house there, she did not approve of Buechner's mother's decision. She thought his mother should "stay and face reality."

But Buechner believes his time in Bermuda played a crucial role in his growth. Bermuda "turned out to be a place where healing could happen in a way that perhaps would not have been possible anywhere else and to a degree that . . . I do not think we would ever have achieved on our own." And of the many gifts Buechner believes he received there, one of the most important was "the gift of forgetting" his father, at least for a time.

Buechner describes his time in Bermuda (the family left not long after Hitler invaded Poland, in September 1939) in vivid and intricate detail: the vehicles, the flowers, the houses, the beaches, the hills. All these and more were "sights and sounds and smells that I had never known before, staggering in their newness."

Naya, Buechner's maternal grandmother, visited the family in Bermuda. Seeing her in this magical new land outside of her usual context made Buechner feel as though he were meeting her all over again. Naya seems to have enjoyed Bermuda as much as Buechner did. By contrast, when Grandmother Buechner visited, she came "like the Inspector General, we feared . . . checking for unreality and extravagance." But she, too, gradually succumbed to the enchanted atmosphere—flirting with the men Buechner's mother introduced to her, for example. "She breathed deep the cedar-laden, salt-sweet air," writes Buechner, "and was as tipsy on it as the rest of us."

## Facing Reality

Near the end of his time in Bermuda, when he was almost thirteen years old, Buechner met a girl about whom he now remembers little except that as their bare knees happened to touch as they sat on a wall watching ferries, he felt "filled with such a sweet panic and anguish of longing for I had no idea what," but he knew his "life could never be complete until [he] found it." He says it was the first time he saw himself as not just someone who could receive love, but someone who could give love, as well.

Looking back on his Bermuda years, Buechner allows that there are other ways of describing and explaining their significance— that they were the result of his natural growth and psychological development, or of the generosity of Grandmother Buechner, or of random chance. But he also chooses not to deny "the compelling sense of an unseen giver and a series of hidden gifts as not only another part of [those years'] reality, but the deepest part of all." For Buechner, those years were and remain an expression of God's grace. They illustrate how "we do well to look back over the journeys of our lives because it is [the hidden gifts'] presence that makes the life of each of us a sacred journey."

## SCRIPTURE REFLECTION

1.  **Ecclesiastes 9:1-12**

    *So I considered all of this carefully, examining all of it: The righteous and the wise and their deeds are in God's hand, along with both love and hate. People don't know anything that's ahead of them. Everything is the same for everyone. The same fate awaits the righteous and the wicked, the good and the bad, the pure and the impure, those who sacrifice and those who don't sacrifice. The good person is like the wrongdoer; the same holds for those who make solemn pledges and those who are afraid to swear. This is the sad thing about all that happens under the sun: the same fate awaits everyone. Moreover, the human heart is full of evil; people's minds are full of madness while they are alive, and afterward they die. Whoever is among the living can be certain about this. A living dog is definitely better off than a dead lion, because the living know that they will die. But the dead know nothing at all. There is no more reward for them; even the memory of them is lost. Their love and their hate, as well as their zeal, are already long gone. They will never again have a stake in all that happens under the sun.*

> *Go, eat your food joyfully and drink your wine*
> *happily because God has already accepted what*
> *you do. Let your garments always be white; don't*
> *run short of oil for your head. Enjoy life with your*
> *dearly loved spouse all the days of your pointless*
> *life that God gives you under the sun—all the days*
> *of your pointless life!—because that's your part to*
> *play in this life and in your hard work under the*
> *sun. Whatever you are capable of doing, do with all*
> *your might because there's no work, thought, knowl-*
> *edge, or wisdom in the grave, which is where you*
> *are headed.*
>
> *I also observed under the sun that the race doesn't*
> *always go to the swift, nor the battle to the mighty,*
> *nor food to the wise, nor wealth to the intelligent,*
> *nor favor to the knowledgeable, because accidents*
> *can happen to anyone. People most definitely don't*
> *know when their time will come. Like fish tragically*
> *caught in a net or like birds trapped in a snare, so*
> *are human beings caught in a time of tragedy that*
> *suddenly falls to them.*

Buechner vividly describes the roulette wheel—"of all things"—
that he and Jamie played with the morning of their father's suicide:
"black and glittery with a chromium spindle at the hub, which it
took only the slightest twirl to set spinning and the little ball skit-
tering clickety-click around the rim . . . On one spin we could be
rich as Croesus.[1] On the next we could lose our shirts."

Roulette wheels are not too far removed from the "wheel of
fortune," the ancient symbol of how we all experience highs and
lows, ups and downs, good and bad as we "roll" through life. It
is a picture that denies any grand pattern or purpose. It's a view

Buechner articulates well toward the end of Chapter 2, as a possible way of interpreting his youth: "What happened happened as much by chance as the chance pattern of raindrops on a windowpane, as much by luck as happening to draw the lucky number in a raffle."

Buechner does *not* ultimately find random chance a sufficient explanation. But neither does he entirely dismiss this view's insight. He asks, "Which of us can look back at our own lives without seeing in them the role of blind chance and dumb luck?" He models how Christians can and should listen to other voices and consider different perspectives while remaining faithful to God, the unseen giver of grace.

Because we Christians tend to think of the Bible as one book (even though "Bible," from the Latin *biblia*, literally means "the books," or library) telling a single story that reaches its climax with Jesus Christ's death and resurrection, we sometimes overlook the diversity of voices within the Bible's own pages.

The book of Ecclesiastes is often a difficult voice for Christians to hear. Its author would understand roulette wheels. He sees the role of "blind chance and dumb luck" in life, as does Buechner, but he doesn't share Buechner's Christian convictions, and he offers no hope that (in Buechner's words) "the best and holiest dream is true after all." But if we make the effort to listen to this author attentively, we may still hear insights that can nurture faith, even if by challenging it.

Jewish and Christian tradition alike have attributed the book to King Solomon on the basis of verses like 1:1,12,16 and 2:9, but the text itself gives only the name Qoheleth, Hebrew for "the Assembler." The title "Ecclesiastes" comes from the Septuagint, the earliest-known Greek translation of Hebrew Scripture (produced in the third and second centuries BCE), and is formed from the Greek word for "assembly," *ekklesia*, the word New Testament authors used for "church." And so this book's author is commonly known in English as "the Teacher" (NRSV, NIV), "the Teacher of the Assembly" (CEB), or "the Preacher" (KJV).

Like Job, Ecclesiastes is Hebrew wisdom literature, dedicated to discerning whatever order God wove into the fabric of creation and to teaching people how to align themselves with that order. Also like Job, Ecclesiastes questions conventional conclusions and traditional teachings about these matters.

But where Job objects to accepted wisdom because it does not explain innocent suffering, Ecclesiastes objects because, as we read in 9:1-12, distinctions between the "wise" and the "foolish" in life—those who live within God's order and those who live outside it—cannot account for the fact that all people ride the wheel of fortune: "time and chance happen to them all" (1:11 NRSV).

The CEB renders the Hebrew word *paga* ("chance," NRSV) as "accidents," which may be a more accurate choice, since the word often occurs in contexts of sudden, violent encounters (see Joshua 2:16; Judges 15:12; 1 Samuel 22:17-18). Qoheleth's point is that no human merit, whether strength or intelligence or wisdom, can fully guard against calamity. Tragic reversals of fortune can and do come without warning. Buechner had no warning his father was about to commit suicide; he simply heard a muffled shout and saw Grandmother Buechner, "fierce and terrified in the hallway," crying out, "Something terrible has happened!" It is a scene Qoheleth would understand.

Qoheleth's comment about chance disasters is one more illustration of a larger theme he has been developing: Death is the great leveler of humankind. As Buechner said in Chapter 1, "Life is terminal." All the delineations we make among ourselves disappear at the grave (9:2-3a). This common fate, more than anything else, lead Qoheleth to conclude that life amounts to "vanity" (9:2 NRSV), a refrain he has been sounding since the book's beginning: "Perfectly pointless.... Everything is pointless" (1:2). The Hebrew word translated as "vanity" (NRSV) or "pointless" (CEB) is *hebel*, and it occurs 38 times in Ecclesiastes. It connotes something fleeting and insubstantial, like a vapor or a shadow; something "without merit," writes scholar W. Sibley Towner, "an unreliable, probably useless thing."[2] Life itself is such a thing, in Qoheleth's considered judgment; it is "a chasing after wind" (1:14).

Why does Qoheleth make this claim? He sees that we spend our lives searching for meaning and purpose in any number of ways, as he did: through pleasure, through learning, through work (Ecclesiastes 2). But whatever we do, we gain nothing lasting and cannot escape mortality. In the current passage, in fact, Qoheleth says the living's only advantage over the dead is that the living know they will die; the dead know nothing (9:5). The dead "exist," if they can be said to exist at all, only in Sheol (9:10), a shadowy afterlife roughly equivalent to the ancient Greek mythological concept of Hades (see the late prophet Samuel's shade in 1 Samuel 28, for instance).

Qoheleth does not deny the presence of order in life. He does not deny that God has a purpose. But he does claim we are unable to discern it (3:11). Confronted with the mysterious intent of this "unseen giver" (to borrow Buechner's phrase), the best we can do is enjoy the gifts. And so Qoheleth advises readers to enjoy "all the days of [their] pointless life" (9:9)—as he says earlier, to "eat, drink, and experience pleasure in their hard work" (2:24)—because that is what God has given mortals to do.

What can Christians make of Qoheleth's message? Although he is not directly interpreting Ecclesiastes in Chapter 2, Buechner may offer some ways forward.

First, Buechner seriously reckons with the reality of death. Although he does (as we will see) share the Christian hope of resurrection, from the moment of his father's suicide he has "ridden on time's back as a man rides a horse, knowing fully that the day will come when my ride will end and my time will end and all that I am and all that I have will end with them." Qoheleth would approve. Christians do not believe death is *the* end, but death is *an* end, and a very real one, overcome by nothing short of a miraculous new beginning from God's own hand. We must give death its due.

And second, Buechner affirms life's goodness in his way as surely as Qoheleth does in his. His rich descriptions of his life in Bermuda convey "the magic and mystery of things"—good gifts of "sights and sounds and smells that [he] had never known before, staggering in their newness." In Bermuda, Buechner learned "there is so much to see always, things too big to take in all at once, things so small as hardly to be noticed." Qoheleth did not share Buechner's sense that the pleasures of life point toward a greater pleasure still, but he would understand Buechner's enjoyment of them, and even affirm them as gifts given by God for us to find pleasurable.

## Questions for Reflection

- When, if ever, have you felt as though your life were like a roulette wheel?
- How easy or difficult do you find Qoheleth's message to hear as a Christian? Why?
- When did you last seriously reflect on the reality of death? How did that experience shape the way you live?

- What are the pleasures of life—the "sights and sounds and smells...staggering in their newness"—in which you take the greatest delight? Why?

2. **Hebrews 1:1-4**

> *In the past, God spoke through the prophets to our ancestors in many times and many ways. In these final days, though, he spoke to us through a Son. God made his Son the heir of everything and created the world through him. The Son is the light of God's glory and the imprint of God's being. He maintains everything with his powerful message. After he carried out the cleansing of people from their sins, he sat down at the right side of the highest majesty. And the Son became so much greater than the other messengers, such as angels, that he received a more important title than theirs.*

In Chapter 2, Buechner suggests that when we Christians speak about *God* speaking, we often do so too quickly, too casually. Discerning exactly how God speaks and what God says is a dominant theme in much of Buechner's work, precisely because God's message to us is "as alive and changing as we are ourselves alive and changing." As Buechner elaborates in his memoir *The Sacred Journey*, God's words to us are "always incarnate words . . . fleshed out in the everydayness no less than in the crises of our own experiences."[3]

The author of the letter to the Hebrews (traditionally identified as the apostle Paul, although the text itself makes no attribution) begins his written sermon, his "message of encouragement"

(13:22), to a dispirited first-century congregation (see, for instance, 3:12-14; 6:11-12; 10:32-39) with a ringing affirmation that, yes, God speaks! Not just once, long ago, through prophets—although certainly God spoke through them (1:1). The same God who spoke to ancient Israel through those messengers has spoken in "these final days... through a Son" (1:2).

Biblical Greek doesn't use capital letters. The CEB, like so many English translations, chooses to capitalize "Son," understandably informed by classic Christian doctrine. But the author of Hebrews isn't teaching fully formed concepts of the Incarnation or the Trinity. He does not say, as John the evangelist does, that God's word (*logos*) became flesh (John 1:14). But he does say that God's communication does not come apart from lived, human experience. If we want to hear God speaking, we must listen for God in this son, this Jesus who died but is now "crowned with glory and honor because of the suffering of his death" (2:9). In this sense, for Hebrews, God's word is an incarnate word, heard clearly in the human life of Jesus, God's son.

Even without the benefit of later Christianity's concept of the Trinity, the author makes clear that this son is not just another prophet. Drawing on ancient Israel's personified portraits of divine wisdom (like that found in Proverbs 8:22-31), the author claims God "created the world" through the son and has made him "heir of everything" (1:2). The son reflects God's glory and is God's *charakter*[4]—the Greek word referred to an engraved mark and came to mean a deep imprint or impression, eventually one's essential quality (thus the English word "character").[5] Here, the author is not far from the Gospel of John, which claims when one has seen Jesus, one has seen God (John 14:8-9).

His descriptions of Jesus also resonate with Colossians 1:15-20, which calls the pre-existent son "the image of the invisible God" through whom and for whom God made everything (Colossians 1:15-16). Hebrews does not articulate Colossians' statement that God's "fullness" is bodily lived in Jesus (Colossians 1:19; 2:9), but the two texts agree that Jesus' death accomplished a reconciliation between heaven and sinful humanity (Colossians 1:20). For the author of Hebrews, however, Jesus accomplished this reconciliation by acting as a priest, cleansing God's covenant people from sin—an image only introduced in 1:3, but later developed in depth (4:14-15; 5:1-10; chapters 8–10).

Neither Buechner nor anyone else could fault the author of Hebrews for speaking "too easily" of God's speech! From the outset, the author prepares his audience for his urgent call to action. God's communication through Jesus is of paramount importance and must be heard: It is "necessary for us to pay more attention to what we have heard"—not less, as this persecuted and weary congregation was apparently tempted to pay—"or else we may drift away from it . . . [and] how will we escape if we ignore such a great salvation?" (2:1, 3).

Buechner doesn't appear to write with the author of Hebrews' conviction that history as a whole is drawing to an end, that first-century Christian certainty, inevitably tempered by two millennia, that we are living "in these final days" (1:2). But Buechner argues that God speaks into our lives with a different but no less real sense of urgency. As he writes in *The Sacred Journey*, "Listen. Your life is happening. You are happening... [God] speaks, I believe, and the words he speaks are incarnate in the flesh and blood of our selves and of our own footsore and sacred journeys."[6]

If we do not listen for God speaking by "look[ing] back over the journeys of our lives," as Buechner does in Chapter 2, we may miss God's crazy and holy gifts of "blessed and blessing moments." We may not hear God's incarnate words to us, or see how they point us toward the son whose life, suffering, and exaltation is God's clearest word.

*Questions for Reflection*
- Which description of Jesus in Hebrews 1:1-4 most arrests your attention, and why?
- How important is it for Christians to affirm that the God who speaks through Jesus is the same God who spoke through the prophets?
- How does listening for God's speech "in the everydayness no less than in the crises of our own experiences" keep us honest when we speak about God?

## PERSONAL RESPONSE

Reflecting on the gap between "the human best" and "the holy best," Buechner alludes to Jesus' "sad joke" about a camel and a needle's eye:

> *Looking around, Jesus said to his disciples, "It will be very hard for the wealthy to enter God's kingdom!" His words startled the disciples, so Jesus told them again, "Children, it's difficult to enter God's kingdom! It's easier for a camel to squeeze through the eye of a needle than for a rich person to enter God's kingdom."*
> *They were shocked even more and said to each other, "Then who can be saved?"*
> *Jesus looked at them carefully and said, "It's impossible with human beings, but not with God. All things are possible for God."*
>
> *Mark 10:23-27*
> *(compare Matthew 19:23-26; Luke 18:24-27)*

Jesus had just told a wealthy man who wanted to know how "to obtain eternal life" (Mark 10:17) that only the man's material possessions stood in his way. If he would sell what he owned and give the proceeds to the poor, Jesus said, he would have "treasure in heaven" (10:21). The rich man, suddenly saddened, either would or could not take that step, prompting Jesus' intentionally exaggerated observation.

The incident is, on its surface (but by no means superficial), about money's powerful potential to become an idol. It is about the way wealth and worldly goods can lure us away from pursuing God's priorities. As Buechner writes elsewhere, maybe people who are rich have a hard time entering God's kingdom "not [because they] are so wicked they're kept out of the place, but that they're so out of touch with reality they can't see it's a place worth getting into."[7]

In these pages, Buechner offers another, broader interpretation. The rich man's problem is that he is "so effective at getting for himself everything he needs that he does not see that what he needs more than anything else in the world can only be had as a gift. He does not see that the one thing a clenched fist cannot do is accept, even from *le bon Dieu* [the good Lord] himself, a helping hand."

Seen from this angle, the story is about not just wealth but whatever we cling to so tightly that we cannot open our hands and hearts to God's crazy, holy grace. Some may clench their fists around their education or their intellect. Others may refuse to let go of preconceived ideas and prejudices about themselves or the world, grimly determined to "face reality," as Grandmother Buechner was. Still others may, as Buechner suggested in Chapter 1, be holding on too much to their pain—all the Miss Havishams of the world.

All of us, in our own ways and to differing degrees, are like the rich man, relying on our human best—our own resources, our own wherewithal—to become the people we know we are meant to be. As Buechner declares, however: "You can survive on your own. You can grow strong on your own. You can even prevail on your own. But you cannot become human on your own."

The good news is that God *can* make us human. God can, and does, do the impossible. God can pry open our clenched fists and our closed hearts so that we can receive all God's gifts.

- What would it sadden you to hear Jesus say he wants you to give up in order to enter the kingdom of God, as the rich man was saddened? Why?
- When, in your own life or others' lives, have you seen God do what is impossible?

# DEVOTION

*Faith is the reality of what we hope for,
the proof of what we don't see. The elders
in the past were approved because they
showed faith.*

It can be humbling to read the "roll call" of our ances-
tors in faith, those brief biographies that fill Hebrews 11
the way sculptures of famous Americans fill Statuary Hall
at the US Capitol.

The letter's author guides us through the exhibition, at
a slow and stately pace at first—here is Abel, here is Enoch,
here is Noah, here is Abraham, and so on—and then more
hurriedly, as though the docents are about to lock up for
the night, for time would fail him to tell of all the rest who
saw God work wonders—or who did not, but suffered for
God's sake all the same.

Perhaps you have not, but I have sometimes wondered:
who am I to think this great cloud of witnesses surrounds
*me*? How is it possible that, as the author of Hebrews rather
improbably insists, that these faithful men and women of
the past won't be made perfect apart from us?

But in my better moments I realize that the author isn't
really interested in showing off "the heroes of the faith"
themselves, but the One in whom they had faith, the One
to whom they looked and trusted with their lives: "Jesus,

faith's pioneer and perfecter" (12:2). They all followed him, each in their own way, throughout their own sacred journeys. Those journeys did not all look alike—except for their steadfast focus on him.

There's an old joke, a flippant saying: "That's my story, and I'm sticking to it." It's usually used when someone can make no rational defense of their position or opinion. But more and more, I'm inclined to think it could also be used as a confession of faith.

It isn't that trust in Jesus is *irrational*, exactly. You can find any number of books, over two millennia of the church's existence, of apologetics, logical arguments defending Christian belief, if you're so inclined. But that trust, that faith, *is* a hope in an unseen reality . . . and this world makes it hard enough to hope in seen realities, let alone unseen ones. We must choose—day by day, moment by moment—to look at our lives through the lens of Jesus' life. It's his story, and we're sticking to it.

If we find we can do that, it's not because we're in any way better than anyone else, any more than our forerunners in faith were. We can only stick to Jesus and his story because, by grace, he has chosen to stick to us first.

*Faithful Lord Jesus, unseen by our physical eyes, we thank you for showing yourself to us all the same, in ways we cannot always explain, but ways that assure us our hope in you is well-placed. Continue to guide us on our journeys, that we, with the great cloud of witnesses, may live with you in this world, and the world you have promised. Amen.*

Session 3

# The Magical
# Room of Memory

# Session 3

# The Magical Room of Memory

## SUMMARY

*"A Room Called Remember"*

In Chapter 3, "A Room Called Remember," Frederick Buechner recounts a dream he once had. In the dream, he was staying in a hotel room where he felt happy and peaceful. The room was named "Remember."

For Buechner, the dream of this room communicates the truth that memory can be healing. Memory can be our own power, rather than external things' and events' power over us.

Buechner argues that we all need to deliberately remember our pasts, both the good and the bad, the pleasure and the pain. We need to take time to remember in order to search for meaning in our lives. Why and how, and for what purpose, have we survived to the present? Buechner compares this kind of remembering to the act of prayer because prayer is also "a search to understand, to hear and be heard." Buechner believes that, in the room called Remember, we discover that we have survived because a strength, a wisdom, and a power beyond our own has pulled us through. We find peace in "looking back and remembering to remember that though most of the time we failed to see it, we were never really alone."

Buechner discusses King David's song of praise in 1 Chronicles 16 as an example of the kind of remembering he means. David remembers, and calls upon ancient Israel to remember, God's wonderful works in the past. Buechner points out that though David could have focused on remembering his own failures, the king instead remembers how God has saved him—and is saving him still, for "salvation itself takes place from day to day." David can show us we have more than our lucky stars to thank for our survival: we have God to thank.

In the room called Remember, we find not only peace but also hope. Because we remember God's past presence with us and power on our behalf, because we realize we have arrived in the present by God's grace, we find more than our best human hopes. We find a "high and holy hope" made manifest in the life of Christ, who encounters us "in countless disguises through people" throughout our lives, and whose "kind of life is the only life that matters." We find the hope that Christ will continue to do the saving work he has been doing, in us and in the world.

## "The Magic of Memory"

In Chapter 4, "The Magic of Memory," Buechner imagines an extended conversation with his dead maternal grandmother, Naya (whom readers will remember having first met in Chapter 2, when she visited Buechner and his family in Bermuda).

In truth, to say Buechner "imagines a conversation" does not do him justice. As he puts it, "I bring Naya into the Magic Kingdom"—his name for his personal library and study. This is the place where he reflects and writes, a room filled with beloved books, photographs, and other special objects, such as a bronze bust of the poet James Merrill, who was Buechner's friend from childhood.[1]

Another special object in the room is a heart-shaped rock Buechner found on a trip to the Farne Islands off the Northumberland coast in England. The stone reminds him of a scene in his novel *Godric* (1980), in which the deceased seventh-century Celtic bishop St. Cuthbert tells the 12th-century hermit Godric, "When a man leaves home, he leaves behind some scrap of his heart. . . . It's the same with a place a man is going to. Only then he sends a scrap of his heart ahead."[2]

Into this room, Buechner "brings" Naya through an act of conscious remembering (and thus a specific example of the kind of remembering Buechner discussed in Chapter 3): "I suspect there is no one on earth, or anywhere else, who cannot really be there if I want them to be and summon them properly."

Buechner talks with Naya about James Merrill's death (in 1995), which made Buechner think more about his own mortality. And so his and Naya's conversation turns to what awaits us after we die. Naya describes death not as the deceased person's "passing away" (a euphemism she does not like), but as *the world's* passing. Death is like stepping off a slowing streetcar, she says: Once passengers have disembarked, the car—the world—goes "rattling off down the tracks" without them.

Naya contrasts life, which is all about "moving on" through space and time, with death, which is "more like moving *in* . . . closer and closer to some new discovery, some revelation that will open up a whole new world, a whole new way of understanding everything."

Buechner contrasts Naya's willingness to "rattle on" about what it is like to be dead with his mother's refusal to contemplate death and what waits beyond it. He remembers one time when she asked him, "Do you really believe anything *happens* after you die?" Because she was so hard of hearing, Buechner ultimately wrote her his answer in a letter. In his letter, he said he believed we are given back our lives for three reasons:

1. He could not believe God wants the people God created to be "consigned to oblivion" before they had become "at least the best they had it in them to be."

2. He believed everyone going to the grave and to nothing after would make life a "black comedy" rather than the "*mystery*" he intuits it is.

3. He believes we are not dead forever "because Jesus said so." He cited Jesus' words to the one thief crucified alongside him as evidence: "Today shalt thou be with me in Paradise" (Luke 23:43, KJV).

Buechner doesn't know whether his mother even read the entire letter, only that she later told him it made her cry, probably because it reminded her of her original question and her own impending death.

He reflects on why he does not bring his mother into his Magic Kingdom and decides it is because he is afraid of her, afraid she will "be too much" for him, as she sometimes was in life. He recalls an argument they had near the end of her life, and the two, seemingly contradictory things she said to him on that occasion: "Why do you hate me?" and "You have always been my hero."

Buechner also concludes that he is afraid of summoning his father back, but for different reasons. Buechner decides his whole life can be seen as a search for his father, yet he is ultimately afraid of finding him and discovering that his father is "too little" for him—or that *he* is "too little" for his father.

## SCRIPTURE REFLECTION

1. **1 Chronicles 16:1-16**

   *They brought in God's chest and placed it inside the tent David had pitched for it. Then they brought entirely burned offerings and well-being sacrifices before God. When David had finished offering the entirely burned offerings and the well-being sacrifices, he blessed the people in the LORD's name and distributed a loaf of bread, a piece of meat, and a raisin cake to every Israelite man and woman.*

   *David appointed some of the Levites to serve before the LORD's chest in order to remember, to give thanks, and to praise the LORD, Israel's God: Asaph was the leader, and Zechariah his assistant; also Jeiel, Shemiramoth, Jehiel, Mattithiah, Eliab, Benaiah, Obed-edom, and Jeiel with harps and lyres; Asaph sounding the cymbals; and the priests Benaiah and Jahaziel blowing trumpets regularly before the chest containing God's covenant. On the same day, for the first time, David ordered Asaph and his relatives to give thanks to the LORD.*

   *Give thanks to the LORD, call on his name;*
   *make his deeds known to all people!*

*Sing to God, sing praises to him;*
*dwell on all his wondrous works!*
*Give praise to God's holy name!*
*Let the hearts rejoice of all those seeking*
*the LORD!*
*Pursue the LORD and his strength;*
*seek his face always!*
*Remember the wondrous works he has done,*
*all his marvelous works,*
*and the justice he declared—*
*you who are the offspring of Israel, his*
*servant,*
*and the children of Jacob, his chosen ones.*
*The LORD—he is our God.*
*His justice is everywhere throughout the*
*whole world.*
*God remembers his covenant forever,*
*the word he commanded to a thousand*
*generations,*
*which he made with Abraham,*
*the solemn pledge he swore to Isaac.*

Because their content covers so much of the same ground as the books of Samuel and Kings cover, the books of Chronicles often suffer neglect from Bible readers, teachers, and preachers. Scholar Leslie C. Allen calls them "the Bible's best-kept secret."[3] Buechner's decision, then, to quote in "A Room Called Remember" from the Chronicler's account of David's bringing of the Ark to Jerusalem, rather than the parallel account in 2 Samuel 6, offers a welcome opportunity to appreciate these books' special perspective.

Dating likely from the early fourth century BCE, Chronicles is itself an extended exercise in the kind of remembering that Buechner calls a deliberate, prayerful searching of the past for meaning and truth.

The Chronicler wrote for a Jewish community that had returned to the Promised Land after decades of exile in Babylon, but even their return was still a kind of exile. The vivid scenes of restoration and refreshment painted by such prophets of the exile as Ezekiel and Second Isaiah (Isaiah 40-55) had not been realized. The Temple in Jerusalem had been rebuilt, but a revived Israel had not united around it and had not achieved the glory the nation had known during the reigns of David and Solomon. The Chronicler addressed a people feeling confused, disillusioned, and even afraid that God was angry with them.

What was the Chronicler's message for the people? This text from 1 Chronicles 16 can serve as a helpful window into it.

First, it is a text about King David. The Chronicler devotes about half of his books to recounting David's and his son Solomon's reigns (1 Chronicles 11–2 Chronicles 9). Like the books of Samuel, Chronicles affirms David as God's specially chosen "shepherd" for Israel (1 Chronicles 11:2). And like the books of Samuel, Chronicles celebrates the eternal covenant God made with David and his family; 1 Chronicles 17 preserves the same divine promise of an eternal "house" for David found in 2 Samuel 7.

But for the Chronicler, David is mainly important because he prepared the way for his son's completion of the Temple, God's "house" on earth. No descendant of David ruled Israel in the Chronicler's day, but a Temple again stood in Jerusalem, representing God's continuing presence with and valid promises to God's people.

And so, in this text, we see David not only bringing the Ark of the Covenant ("God's chest," 16:1; the box that contained the tablets of the Law given to Moses) to Jerusalem, his capital city, but we also see him establishing patterns of worship that would continue in the Temple. David appoints some of the Levites—descendants of Jacob's son, Levi, set apart by God for priestly service (Numbers 3:11-12)—"to remember, to give thanks, and to praise the LORD, Israel's God" through music (16:4-6).

When quoting this text in his essay, Buechner omits verses 5-6. But these Levites' names deserve to be remembered (even the ones non-Hebrew speakers might find tricky to pronounce!), since their musical ministry was, in part, a ministry of memory. And David charged them to help Israel remember God's grace. He told them to sing so the people would not forget, in Buechner's words, that God "has been with us through all our days and years whether we knew it or not."

Chronicles teaches, as do the books of Samuel, that God rewards obedience and punishes disobedience (see, for instance, the story of David's census in 1 Chronicles 21). But it also stresses God's grace. The Levites' song illustrates this emphasis. It is actually made up of portions from Psalms 105, 96, and 106 (all of which biblical scholars date to after the Babylonian Exile), but the unifying element is, as Buechner notes, joyful thanksgiving for all that God has done in the past (16:8-10). It is a song about God's salvation, which began with the eternal and unbreakable covenant with Abraham (16:15-16) and will reach into the future, to the day when God finally and fully "establish[es] justice on earth!" (16:33). Just as Buechner explains, the remembrance of God's activity in the past yields to hopeful anticipation of God's activity in the future.

Far from ignoring the gap between his people's days and the days of David and Solomon, or the gap between his people's high expectations and their currently painful reality, the Chronicler focuses on the element in their present—the Temple—that connects God's history with them to God's plans for them. He would understand Buechner's conclusion that faith is all about remembering and waiting in hope.

*Questions for Reflection*

- When you "dwell on all [God's] wondrous works" (16:9), what do you think about, and why?
- What music helps you remember and give thanks to God (16:4)?
- How can remembering be a ministry, a service, to God and to other people?

2. **Luke 23:39-43**

> *One of the criminals hanging next to Jesus insulted him: "Aren't you the Christ? Save yourself and us!"*
> *Responding, the other criminal spoke harshly to him, "Don't you fear God, seeing that you've also been sentenced to die? We are rightly condemned, for we are receiving the appropriate sentence for what we did. But this man has done nothing wrong." Then he said, "Jesus, remember me when you come into your kingdom."*
> *Jesus replied, "I assure you that today you will be with me in paradise."*

Twice in these chapters, Buechner mentions Jesus' promise to the so-called "Good Thief," who is crucified alongside him. Although both mentions are brief, they communicate significant truths about God for him. First, in Chapter 3, Buechner points to the story to urge readers to "Remember him who himself remembers us. . . . " Then, in Chapter 4, he includes the story in his letter to his mother: "I believe that what happens to us after we die is that we aren't dead forever because Jesus said so."

Despite the common custom of organizing Good Friday services or musical performances around the "Seven Last Words from the Cross," none of the four Gospels records all seven sayings. Instead, each Evangelist tells the story of Jesus' crucifixion in a way that reflects his and his community's particular theological interests. Each offers a portrait of Jesus that, while not completely unrelated to the others, lifts up truths about his death and his identity that combinations of more than one may obscure.

For Luke, Jesus is a Savior for all people who nonetheless provokes sharp division. Consider Luke's story of Jesus' birth, for instance. When Joseph and Mary present the infant Jesus in the Temple, Simeon tells them the child is both "a light for revelation to the Gentiles" (non-Jewish peoples) and "a glory for [God's] people Israel" (2:32); however, within Israel, Jesus will become "the cause of the falling and rising of many" and "a sign that generates opposition" (2:34).

As Luke traces Jesus' life and public ministry, we see Simeon's prophecy fulfilled at several moments, including this one just before Jesus' death. Both Mark and Matthew report that the criminals crucified with him mocked him (Mark 15:32; Matthew 27:44). But according to Luke, only one criminal scorns Jesus. In fact, Luke literally says this criminal "blasphemed" (*eblasphēmei*). He ironically confesses Jesus' divine status—the truth that, as Buechner says, Jesus "in one way... was a human being, [but] in another way . . . was immeasurably more"—and Jesus' right to the title "Christ" (Greek for "anointed one," and so equivalent to the Hebrew "messiah") even as he mocks him.

In contrast, the other criminal confesses Jesus' innocence (as the Roman centurion will when Jesus breathes his last [23:47]) and takes seriously Jesus' ability to save him—not from his imminent physical death, as the first criminal cynically had, but for a place in Jesus' future kingdom. Hanging between the two, Jesus is literally, as he dies, dividing Israel, just as Simeon foretold.

The second criminal asks Jesus to remember him. Hebrew Scripture offers many examples of people in distress calling out for God to remember them, including Hannah (1 Samuel 1:11), Jeremiah (15:15), and the psalm-singers (Psalm 106:4). God "remembered" Noah after the Flood (Genesis 8:1), Abraham after the destruction of Sodom and Gomorrah (Genesis 19:29), and Rachel when she wanted to conceive (Genesis 30:22). Buechner is right to speak of God as the one who remembers us, and the second criminal is right to request that same saving act of remembrance from Jesus.

Jesus grants that request—and more. The criminal will not have to wait to be with Jesus, but will be with him "today" in "Paradise" (Luke 23:43). "Paradise" is an uncommon word in the Bible. Deriving ultimately from an ancient Iranian source word for a walled-in garden or park,[19] it is what the Septuagint (the Greek translation of Hebrew Scripture) calls the Garden of Eden. In the New Testament, it appears only three times: here, 2 Corinthians 12:4 (the apostle Paul's reluctant, roundabout description of his own ecstatic visions), and Revelation 2:7 (the risen Jesus promises believers who endure persecution will eat from "the tree of life, which is in God's paradise").

What do Jesus' words mean when placed alongside other New Testament texts that picture resurrection from the dead as the second criminal thought of it, a future event? Paul spoke of it so, in 1 Corinthians 15 and 1 Thessalonians 4:13-18—although he also told the Philippians he wrestled with a desire "to leave this life and be with Christ" (Philippians 1:23). We probably do better to treat every biblical image of the next life on its own, just as we should, at least sometimes, treat each Gospel's portrait of Jesus on its own.

Taken on their own, Jesus' words to the thief communicate what Buechner told his mother they do: they are an authoritative promise that death is not the end, because Jesus "of all people knew what he was talking about." And they reinforce Luke's portrait of Jesus: the Jewish Messiah who, by his very presence, divides his people, but who willingly extends salvation to anyone who will humbly trust him.

*Questions for Reflection*
- Why did Jesus prove divisive during his life and ministry? To what extent is Jesus still "a sign that generates opposition"?
- How do you respond to the image of life after death as Paradise?
- What do you mean when you call Jesus "Savior"?

## PERSONAL RESPONSE

In Chapter 4, Buechner recalls the way he answered his mother's question, "Do you really believe anything *happens* after you die?" Because his mother was hard of hearing, Buechner shouted his initial response—"YES . . . SOMETHING HAPPENS"—but then later wrote his answer in a letter, because "there are things that cannot be shouted."

The apostle Paul wrote a letter in which (among other matters) he tried to answer early Christians' questions about what happens after death. Apparently, some believers in Corinth were doubting the idea that God would raise the dead on the last day, an expectation that had become part of many Jews' faith by the first century (as we see in Martha's conversation with Jesus in John 11:23-27).

Whether Paul would have shouted his response had he been face-to-face with his readers, we don't know (although, given Paul's personality, it doesn't seem a far-fetched idea). But he does emphatically make his case in 1 Corinthians 15:12-28:

> So if the message that is preached says that Christ has been raised from the dead, then how can some of you say, "There's no resurrection of the dead"? If there's no resurrection of the dead, then Christ hasn't been raised either. If Christ hasn't been raised, then our preaching is useless and your faith is useless. We are found to be false witnesses about God, because we testified against God that he raised Christ, when he didn't raise him if it's the case that the dead aren't raised. If the dead aren't raised, then Christ hasn't been raised either. If Christ hasn't been raised, then your faith is worthless; you are still in your sins, and what's more, those who have died in Christ are gone forever. If we have a hope in Christ only in this life, then we deserve to be pitied more than anyone else.
>
> But in fact Christ has been raised from the dead. He's the first crop of the harvest of those who have died. Since death came through a human being, the resurrection of the dead came through one too. In the same way that everyone dies in Adam, so also everyone will be given life in Christ. Each event will happen in the right order: Christ, the first crop

*of the harvest, then those who belong to Christ at his coming, and then the end, when Christ hands over the kingdom to God the Father, when he brings every form of rule, every authority and power to an end. It is necessary for him to rule until he puts all enemies under his feet. Death is the last enemy to be brought to an end, since he has brought everything under control under his feet. When it says that everything has been brought under his control, this clearly means everything except for the one who placed everything under his control. But when all things have been brought under his control, then the Son himself will also be under the control of the one who gave him control over everything so that God may be all in all.*

While we might understand why someone would doubt Jesus' resurrection—people don't return from the dead every day, after all, and rare is the Christian who has never, at some point, wrestled with doubts about this core claim of the faith—Paul's readers *weren't* questioning Jesus' new life. They were questioning the idea that his resurrection implied anything about their own.

For Paul, Jesus' resurrection itself validates the belief that God will raise the dead at the end of all things. The first Easter was not a supernatural fluke. As important as it is (and it is "most important," 1 Corinthians 15:3), it is the prelude, the overture to what is yet to come. Paul used an agricultural metaphor familiar from Israel's history: The risen Jesus is "the first fruits of those who have died" (15:20 NRSV). His resurrection life is the "first taste" God gives of our own.

Paul only considers the alternative for argument's sake (15:13-19). Buechner is in excellent company, then, when he writes in the letter to his mother that he cannot believe life is a "black comedy," some kind of grim and cynical farce where we "all end up alike in the grave and that is the end of it." With Paul, Buechner says no to this possibility.

Paul argues that nothing less than God's authority is at stake in this question of what happens after we die. Death is the final enemy (15:26)—the sole holdout resisting God's good will for the whole creation, including the human race. God's will is to be "all in all" (15:28). If the dead are not raised, God's will would be forever frustrated. But Jesus' resurrection proves otherwise. He has in fact been raised, Paul proclaims (15:20), and so all God's enemies are, in effect, on borrowed time. They will all ultimately be put under God's feet (15:25).

Terrible, tragic, anxiety-producing headlines sometimes prompt Christians to ask, "Are we living in the end times?" For Paul, the answer to that question is, "Yes"—not because the world's news is ever so bad as to suggest that God is not in control, but because the news of Jesus' resurrection is so *good* as to remove any doubt that God reigns. We have been "living in the end times" since that morning at Jesus' empty tomb 2,000 years ago. And because we are, we have "the sure and certain hope" (as the *Book of Common Prayer* puts it)[5] that what happens after we die—whatever images and metaphors we use to describe it—will be good.

Arguably, this truth, like the truth Buechner wanted to tell his mother, is not heard best as a shout. We must give the apparent evidence to the contrary to its due, because it is sometimes overwhelming. But it is a truth we have been given to say somehow, and we must, so that we and others can know and believe, in Buechner's words, that "at the innermost of heart of [life], there is Holiness."

- How would you have answered the question Buechner's mother asked him?
- What do you do when you have questions or doubts about what happens after we die, or about the claim, "Christ has been raised from the dead"?
- What is one way, in word or in action, that you will tell someone this week the good news Christians have to tell about what happens after we die?

## DEVOTION

*I'm sure about this: the one who started a good work in you will stay with you to complete the job by the day of Christ Jesus.*

*Philippians 1:6*

Sometimes it's only in retrospect, in remembering, that we see the shape of God's day-to-day work in our lives. When I look back over my life for examples of how God has been working in and working on me, I think back to the time, about a dozen years ago now, when I fell and broke my right leg.

I say I broke it. The doctors said I "shattered" it. I'd been hurrying to a city bus stop on a winter morning and stepped in a snow-covered storm drain, catching my foot. I could hear the bones snapping as I fell forward. The break was serious, but in just the right places that the surgeons could fix it with a plate and twelve screws. I'd actually been lucky. My wife and I later joked that, had I fallen and broken my leg in that way back in the days of nomadic hunter-gatherers, my tribe probably would have left me behind.

But as I started what would be a difficult week of physical therapy following the surgery, I had never felt so demoralized. One of my first assigned tasks was to stand at a table for ten minutes on my one good, weight-bearing leg. Those ten minutes felt like ten hours. As the days in therapy passed, I made physical progress, but I continued to wrestle with discouragement and anger.

Then an editor with whom I was working on a project before my accident said something to me that helped me see my situation in a new way. "You know," she said, "there's a lot of things you can't do with a broken leg, but you can still write for God."

Her words spurred me to start thinking of my physical misstep as a step in the right direction. After seven years as the pastor of a congregation, I had recently decided to resign in order to get a "regular, 9-to-5 job" that would leave me time and energy to focus on building a ministry of writing. But moving on emotionally and spiritually from pastoral ministry had been proving more difficult than I expected. In fact, the very week of my accident, only a few months into my new job, I'd agreed to take on an eight-Sunday commitment as a substitute preacher.

Well, my newly limited mobility meant cancelling those plans. But my editor's words helped me intuit something deeper that was happening. Did God cause me to fall? Of course not. But now I was seeing that I could not continue to straddle the past and the present. If I was going to leave pastoral ministry behind for something else, I needed really to leave it behind, in order to see where God would lead. I started seeing my broken leg as a literal break with my previous profession that freed me to embrace my new one, my ministry of "writing for God."

I kept working to move from a walker to crutches to a cane to my own two feet. Nothing about my recovery was supernatural, but each milestone I reached felt miraculous. And I walked away from the experience with a stronger sense that Jesus always walks with me, and that God is at work within us—as individuals, and as the body of Christ—to bring God's good will for us to completion.

Frederick Buechner wrote to his mother that he couldn't believe God would abandon people until they had become "at last the best they had it in them to be." My experience leads me to believe the same thing. God doesn't leave important jobs unfinished. God will, day by day, save us from becoming anything less than the people God wants us to be.

*Loving God, we thank you for your commitment to us. We thank you for your tenacious grace that refuses to give up on us. By your Spirit, keep us walking with you, and move us to welcome the good work you have begun within us and will finally bring to completion by the day of Jesus Christ. Amen.*

Session 4

# The Struggle and Hope of Memory

# Session 4

# The Struggle and Hope of Memory

## SUMMARY

*"The Struggle of Memory"*

As he continues his imagined conversation with Naya in the "Magic Kingdom" of his library, Buechner asks her if she believed in God during her life, and if she is a believer now that she is dead. She says she "always believed . . . that there was more than met the eye" in life, and that death did not solve all mysteries but "was like stepping out of a dark house into the greater dark of night." Similarly, Naya does not claim she has definitively seen Jesus, but that she will know him if she does by his quiet, "kingly tread." Buechner tells Naya that Jesus will know her.

He then reflects on his brother, Jamie, who died just shy of his seventieth birthday. He strives to capture Jamie's face in words, but he is also concerned with putting the inner man on the page. Jamie was a private person, an unassuming and unpretentious man who always "took life as it came instead of, like [Buechner], brooding about the past or worrying himself sick about the future." Buechner says that whenever his brother laughed, he gave "the richest and the best of himself that he had to give."

While Frederick made Jamie's life "miserable," as big brothers often do, when they were young boys, their father's suicide brought them together in a powerful way. Buechner recounts again the story of how he found Jamie weeping over their father's death a year after it happened. Jamie grieved the loss of their father much sooner than Buechner did; consequently, their father's suicide did not haunt Jamie as it has haunted Buechner.

Buechner describes his brother's enjoyment of language (he wrote little poems in Buechner's guest book, for example), and also his ingenuity with electronics. He describes how Jamie matter-of-factly accepted his terminal cancer, and how he saw him for the last time during "a brief, hectic visit" to New York City. They said goodbye to each other by phone in 1998, after having talked almost daily during the final two weeks of Jamie's life. He hopes that it is true that he and his brother have not seen the last of each other.

### "The Hope of Memory"

Buechner once tried using a Ouija board to write out a conversation between him and his father. In that conversation, his father told him not to be afraid for or worried about him: "There's nothing to worry about. That's the secret I never knew, but I know it now . . . I know plenty, and it's all good."

When he tries to summon Jamie, as he has summoned Naya, he sees him for only a moment. Naya laughs at him for dismissing what he sees as "*only* a vision . . . *only* a dream." She suggests that he is glimpsing "what God has prepared for those who love him"

(1 Corinthians 2:9 NRSV). When Buechner presses her for details about what God *has* prepared, she tells him that mystery is "deeper and grander than [she] ever supposed." She says it is "we ourselves that [God's] preparing," both those who love God and those who do not. She tells him the more she sees in death, the more she realizes she has yet to see—but that everything she sees is good. Naya assures him that Jamie is there, and "will find himself," for no one and nothing is ever lost. When Buechner thanks her for what she has told him, she urges him to remember, "I am a dream, but I am not only a dream."

Buechner wants to believe what Naya says is true—that we will find our true selves after death—and ponders the fact that, even as he grows older in this life, he finds himself less concerned with what others think and more concerned with being true to who he is. The benefits of responding authentically to other people in life's moments far outweigh the risks, he decides. In these interactions, even if they are only fleeting, and with people he does not even know except in limited contexts, he feels most himself.

All the same, he is struck by how he has, in his judgment, been "timorous" about revealing himself in his four books of autobiography, and how he has been reticent and roundabout in writing about his Christian hope "for fear of losing the ear and straining the credulity of the readers to whom such hope seems just wishful thinking." Is he afraid, he wonders, of saying too much about his faith for fear of losing people's respect or friendship? In his novels, he decides, he has expressed several autobiographical moments of faith through his characters, even if he has not lived the life of "holy recklessness" that should flow from such experiences.

As this chapter and book draw to a conclusion, Buechner tells the story of how he was on an airplane flying through turbulence. He remembered two things: Deuteronomy 33:27 (KJV)—

"underneath are the everlasting arms," an assuring image of security in God, even "if [Buechner's] worst fears were realized"—and a Buddhist metaphor about people being clay jars that are broken throughout life until only its emptiness remains, "the only thing about it that is ultimately so real that nothing on earth or heaven has the power to touch it, let alone destroy it." This emptiness is not Nothingness, but is joined with all other jars' emptiness and is "whatever of its many names we call it by—nirvana, satori, eternal life, the peace of God." With these thoughts in his mind, Buechner knew: "yes, it was true. There was nothing to worry about. There was no reason to fear. It was all of it, *all* of it, and forever and always, good."

Alone in his "Magic Kingdom," Buechner reveals its true enchantment: "if you look at it through the right pair of eyes it points to a kingdom more magic still," the New Jerusalem described in Revelation 21-22.

## SCRIPTURE REFLECTION

1. **Ephesians 1:15-23**

   *Since I heard about your faith in the Lord Jesus and your love for all God's people, this is the reason that I don't stop giving thanks to God for you when I remember you in my prayers. I pray that the God of our Lord Jesus Christ, the Father of glory, will give you a spirit of wisdom and revelation that makes God known to you. I pray that the eyes of your heart will have enough light to see what is the hope of God's call, what is the richness of God's glorious inheritance among believers, and what is the overwhelming greatness of God's power that is working among us believers. This power is conferred by the energy of God's powerful strength. God's power was at work in Christ when God raised him from the dead and sat him at God's right side in the heavens, far above every ruler and authority and power and angelic power, any power that might be named not only now but in the future. God put everything under Christ's feet and made him head of everything in the church, which is his body. His body, the church, is the fullness of Christ, who fills everything in every way.*

Buechner finds the phrase in Ephesians 1:18, "the eyes of your heart," to be "words where [he] never found them before and just when [he] needed them." They come to signify, for Buechner, a way of glimpsing in the world, in one's own life, evidence of the hope to which Christian faith points—not ironclad, forensic evidence that would hold up in a court of law, but evidence that persuades him to believe that "there is nothing to worry about, not even death, not even life," and that "no one is ever really lost."

He provides a summation of the personal hope proclaimed in Ephesians 1. And when we review the context in which the phrase "the eyes of your heart" occurs, we may appreciate how that hope is even more expansive.

As Buechner acknowledges in passing, the letter to the Ephesians, traditionally attributed to the apostle Paul, may well have been written by someone else in Paul's name. The use of a pseudonym wasn't uncommon in ancient letters, and literary scholars have established that audiences then wouldn't have regarded the practice as deceptive or fraudulent the way modern readers do now. Instead, invoking Paul's name and authority shows the writer is attempting to engage a new situation in the way

Paul himself might have. The writer takes cues from Paul's own teaching and preaching. Certainly, Ephesians' emphasis on unity between Jewish and Gentile believers in Jesus (see 2:11-22; 3:8; 4:4-6) agrees with Paul's understanding of himself as the apostle to the Gentiles (for example, Galatians 1:15-16; Romans 15:18-21). And, as Buechner notes, the writer's prayer that God would grant his readers a spirit of revelation (Ephesians 1:17) "is just about what you would expect [Paul] to ask."

The phrase that arrests Buechner so, "the eyes of the heart," appears nowhere else in the Bible. But scholar Pheme Perkins notes that Hebrew Scripture frequently identifies the heart as "the seat of human understanding," and cites other Jewish texts that "refer to the darkened or clouded eye as equivalent to a depraved will."[1] The author is praying for the readers' moral enlightenment. He is praying for both their new sight and their new direction. A clear vision of Christian hope calls for clear changes in Christian conduct. Buechner, in fact, goes on to address this connection between hope and behavior when he confesses that "to live the kind of life that you would expect to flow from [what he has seen and experienced of God] passes beyond risk into a kind of holy recklessness that is beyond" him.

We will assume here that the author of Ephesians is Paul. Paul does put forth a grand, sweeping vision of hope. The letter begins with one of those "long and tangled" sentences for which Naya criticizes Paul: Chapter 1, verses 3-14 are a single sentence in the original Greek, so dense and dazzling that English translators have no choice but to break it up into several. It declares, objectively, that God has blessed believers "with every spiritual blessing that comes from heaven" (1:3). It locates the moment of salvation not in some moment of decision on the readers' parts, but "before the creation of the world" (1:4), when God "destined" them to be God's "adopted children" (1:5). And it connects the readers' conversions to the ultimate destiny of everything, for God has "planned for the climax of all times: to bring all things together in Christ" (1:10). Paul puts the readers' experience of faith against a breathtaking, universal backdrop.

Then Paul prays, in the verses from which Buechner quotes, that his readers will be given the ability to share that vision. He prays their hearts' eyes will "have enough light" to see it with him (1:18)—to see not only what God has already done for them in its proper, cosmic perspective but also what God is still doing for and in and through them. God's "power"—the Greek word is *dynameōs*,[2] and it might not be wrong to think of "dynamite" used for constructive, rather than destructive, ends—is working among them, the same divine dynamite that raised Jesus from death, lifting him to supremacy over all other powers, present or future (1:20-21; compare 6:12).

Although Buechner—appropriately enough in an autobiographical volume—focuses on the personal, quiet, individual moments in which the eyes of his heart have seen flashes of this reality, the text of Ephesians maintains a focus on the church. The church is not just Christ's body on earth; it is also "the fullness of Christ, who fills everything in every way" (1:23). The text insists the church experiences a unique connection to the risen Christ and is filled to overflowing with God's life-giving might.

In effect, Paul is asking his readers: "Can you all see yourselves this way, as I see you all—more important, as *God* sees you all? Can your hearts' eyes see the amazing, universe-filling power that fills your community, too? And if so—what will you say and do as a result? What kind of life will you now live, to respond to the great hope to which God has called us?" Our rich inheritance in Christ (1:18) is not meant to be hoarded away for the future world. It is abundant enough that we must be spending it now, in speech and deeds empowered by God that point others toward the one who already fills all things.

*Questions for Reflection*

- Talk about a time when your hope as a Christian prompted you to speak or act in a new and different way. What happened?
- Do you tend to think about your Christian hope for the future in individual terms or in terms of the church and the world? Why?
- How would you describe the degree to which your church believes itself to be filled to overflowing with the same power of God that raised Jesus? Why?
- The author of Ephesians is praying for his readers. For whom do you pray that God would open their hearts' eyes? What do you want God to show them? How might God show them that sight through you?

2. **1 Corinthians 2:6-16**

*What we say is wisdom to people who are mature. It isn't a wisdom that comes from the present day or from today's leaders who are being reduced to nothing. We talk about God's wisdom, which has been hidden as a secret. God determined this wisdom in advance, before time began, for our glory. It is a wisdom that none of the present-day rulers have understood, because if they did understand it, they would never have crucified the Lord of glory! But this is precisely what is written: God has prepared things for those who love him that no eye has* seen, or ear has heard, or that haven't crossed the mind of any human being. *God has revealed these things to us through the Spirit. The Spirit searches everything, including the depths of God. Who knows a person's depths except their own spirit that lives in them? In the same way, no one has known the depths of God except God's Spirit. We haven't received the world's spirit but God's Spirit so that we can know the things given to us by God. These are the things we are talking about—not with words taught by human wisdom but with words taught by the Spirit—we are interpreting spiritual things to spiritual people. But people who are unspiritual don't accept the things from God's Spirit. They are foolishness to them and can't be understood, because they can only be comprehended in a spiritual way. Spiritual people comprehend everything, but they themselves aren't understood by anyone.* Who has known the mind of the Lord, who will advise him? *But we have the mind of Christ.*

One of the surprises Naya has for Buechner as they converse in his "Magic Kingdom" is the revelation that some surprises and secrets still await us after we die. Buechner asks her, "What *has* [God] prepared for those who love him, then?"—a direct quotation of 1 Corinthians 2:9. But Naya can only tell him that, defying her own expectations, this mystery "is not only [still] a mystery but deeper and grander than [she] ever supposed." She can only tell her grandson that God is preparing people, both those who love God and those "who don't care a fig about him one way or the other."

First Corinthians 2:9 is itself already a quotation. The apostle Paul (and, unlike in the case of Ephesians, scholars have no doubt that Paul himself wrote the Corinthian epistles) is quoting Isaiah 64:4, a verse that references God's remembered actions for Israel. The prophet prays that God would again make the divine presence and power known and felt as in the past: "When you accomplished wonders beyond all our expectations; when you came down, mountains quaked before you. From ancient times, no one has heard, no ear has perceived, no eye has seen any god but you who acts on behalf of those who wait for him!" (64:3-4). Isaiah doesn't explicitly mention the Exodus, but his talk of quaking mountains evokes the scene of the LORD descending upon Mount Sinai (Exodus 19:18-20). Whatever specific events he may have in mind, Isaiah is praying for a performance of a miraculous intervention on Israel's behalf the likes of which the world had not seen before.

As so many devout and learned rabbis have (including Jesus), Paul "plays" with the divinely inspired text of Scripture in a midrash. Modern academics would say Paul is taking the verse out of context. He is. But he does so in order to tease new meaning out of the ancient words for his and his readers' situation. And so, in Paul's interpretation, Isaiah 64:4 is not about what no one had seen or heard *before*, but about what anyone *has yet* to see or hear. The words point not backward to what God has done but forward to what God will do. They are not about the past but about the future.

But Paul only makes this point to address his present. All these unseen, unheard, unknown realities God is preparing for those who love God? "God has revealed these things to us"—already, here and now—"through the Spirit" (1 Corinthians 2:10).

Paul's point, then, is very unlike Naya's. So far from remaining a deeper and grander mystery, God's will is graciously disclosed to the "mature" (2:6), to "spiritual people" (2:13)—in other words, to baptized members of the body of Christ (1 Corinthians 1:13-16;

12:12-13). The word "Christian" was not yet in use in Paul's time. For Paul, only "people who are unspiritual" fail to understand what God's Spirit reveals.

The apostle draws a sharp dividing line. He proposes a strict "either/or": People either have the mind of the world or "the mind of Christ" (2:16). He might be surprised, then, maybe even scandalized, by Naya's "report" from beyond death that she hasn't seen more of the mystery, that she hasn't even necessarily seen Jesus. (Of course, Naya never cared much for Paul—"that old sinner," she calls him—so she wouldn't be bothered by his disapproval!)

In order to appreciate Paul's perspective, which could seem to be a theological "us vs. them," we have to remember that he wasn't setting out to write a systematic theology. He was a pastor, and his letters never engage in the kind of free-flowing, prayerfully imaginative daydreaming by which Buechner conjures Naya. The congregations to which Paul wrote all faced practical problems, and Paul was interested in thinking his way to practical solutions for them.

The believers in first-century Corinth were a disorganized and divided lot. Paul leads off this letter to them by lamenting how they have split up into "rival groups" (1:10). In quick succession, he chastises them for tolerating sexual immorality in their midst (5:1-13), for dragging each other to Roman courts (6:1-11), for indulging their Christian freedom at the expense of their fellow believers' consciences (8:1-13), and for letting the economic gap between the poor and the rich stain their celebrations of the Lord's Supper (11:17-34). In all these matters, Paul is upset that he can't deal with the Corinthians as the "spiritual people" they objectively are by virtue of baptism (12:13); he has to treat them like the "unspiritual people" they've chosen, by their behaviors, to become (3:1).

So 1 Corinthians 2:9 is not, primarily, a verse about what happens after we die. It is a verse about Christians acting like Christians while they are alive! Paul is imploring the community of faith to reclaim its God-given identity as "spiritual people" before their worldly behavior jeopardizes it beyond recovery.

In this respect, if in no other, Paul might agree with Naya: whatever God may be preparing for us in the hereafter, God is preparing us to be the people we were meant to be. We all need help becoming human, and most of all we need the helping hand of God.

This preparation for becoming who we were always meant to be may well continue after we die, for, as Naya tells Buechner, "no one is lost." We saw in Session 3 that Paul says much the same thing later in 1 Corinthians: God will bring "everything under control under [Christ's] feet" (15:27). And, as he writes in *The Sacred Journey*, those who have died

> have their own business to get on with now, I assume— "increasing in knowledge and love of Thee," says the Book of Common Prayer, and moving "from strength to strength," which sounds like business enough for anybody.[3]

Saint Paul, Naya, Jamie Buechner, Frederick Buechner himself (God willing, no day too soon), you reading this book, me writing it—we will die, all of us, but we will not be lost in that place (in Buechner's words) "where we find our true selves at last and also the truth of each other and of the mystery at last."

*Questions for Reflection*

- When, like Isaiah, have you longed for God to act in undeniable ways that all people can see, hear, and know?

- How do you react to Paul's division of "spiritual" and "unspiritual" people?
- What does "having the mind of Christ" look like in practical, everyday ways in the individual believer's life? In the life of the Christian community?

## PERSONAL RESPONSE

Despite Buechner's self-assessment of how he has borne witness to Christ—"only obliquely, hesitantly, ambiguously"—the story of his turbulent plane ride that closes the book makes clear that, whatever doubts and questions with which he still wrestles, he believes the hope he has glimpsed with the eyes of his heart, that no one is lost and that all is ultimately good. He believes in "eternal life" (for him, one of "its many names we call it by").

At the beginning of the First Letter of John, the writer tells his readers:

> *We announce to you what existed from the beginning, what we have heard, what we have seen with our eyes, what we have seen and our hands handled, about the word of life. The life was revealed, and we have seen, and we testify and announce to you the eternal life that was with the Father and was revealed to us. What we have seen and heard, we also announce it to you so that you can have fellowship with us. Our fellowship is with the Father and with his Son, Jesus Christ. We are writing these things so that our joy can be complete.*
>
> *1 John 1:1-4*

He does not quote 1 John here, but Buechner's and the apostle's bases for their respective testimonies seem similar. Neither one presumes to talk about truths they have not personally heard with their own ears, seen with their own eyes, or touched with their own hands, even if only in some sporadic and fragmentary way. Whether fully or partially, whether often or occasionally, "[t]he life was revealed," and they have seen it (1:2). And both say whatever they believe they can honestly say about it in order to complete their joy, and that others may share that joy with them.

- How much do you agree with Buechner's evaluation of his witness to Christ? Why?
- When, if ever, have you been "hesitant" or "ambiguous" in your own witness?
- How does limiting what we proclaim about Christ to what we have experienced for ourselves keep us honest and humble in our testimony?
- How does the collective testimony of the church supplement our own individual testimonies?
- What is the simplest, most honest proclamation you can make about your own belief in the Christian hope of eternal life?

# DEVOTION

*Then I saw a new heaven and a new
earth, for the former heaven and the former
earth had passed away, and the sea was no
more. I saw the holy city, New Jerusalem,
coming down out of heaven from God,
made ready as a bride beautifully dressed
for her husband. I heard a loud voice from
the throne say, "Look! God's dwelling is
here with humankind. He will dwell with
them, and they will be his peoples. God
himself will be with them as their God. He
will wipe away every tear from their eyes.
Death will be no more. There will be no
mourning, crying, or pain anymore, for the
former things have passed away." Then the
one seated on the throne said, "Look! I'm
making all things new." He also said, "Write
this down, for these words are trustworthy
and true."*

*Revelation 21:1-5*

Naya tells Buechner she used to hear these words "at
some poor soul's funeral" in Calvary Church and, because
they were "so lovely," she "could almost believe they were
true."

I can empathize with Naya's emotional reaction to these
words. Growing up in a congregation fortunate enough

to have (or, perhaps, simply with immodest amounts of money to spend on) a large and active music program, I came to love a certain musical setting of Revelation, an anthem by composer David Danner entitled, "Arise, Your Light Has Come."

If you've never heard it, you should find a recording and listen to it. It's an incredible arrangement of the old Lutheran chorale *"Wachet Auf"* ("Sleepers Awake"). When performed in all its magnificence, it's full of pipe organ and strings and horns and handbells and rich four-part harmony. It's a long piece; the choir I listened to, and eventually sang with before I moved away, performed an abbreviated version that still ran nearly six minutes. And it builds and builds in beauty and boldness until, by the time you're singing the part about the New Jerusalem with its shining pearl portals, tears are streaming down your face— or at least they did mine, and still do.

But now, several decades later, I weep at that piece for different reasons.

As a young man, even up to the time I entered seminary straight out of college, I thought it was the perfect musical setting of the Apocalypse's final, dazzling vision. It sounded like the swelling and soaring orchestral movie music I've always adored. Others in the choir and even in my family found it bombastic, but I thought, "Well, if it's bombastic, so be it! It's a song about the final triumph of God, who is making all things new. If you can't be bombastic about a subject like that, when can you?"

But today, while I am not old (at least not in my own mind—ask my children, you'll get a different answer), I am *older*. I have felt pain in my own life and heart and seen it in the lives and hearts of others more frequently than I did as a young man. I've grown more aware of the crushing pain and maddening injustices that plague our country and the world. And there are days when the vision John saw and shared seems like "wishful thinking" at best, and a callous joke at worst.

Every tear wiped away? An end to death? No more mourning, or crying, or pain, at all? Who can imagine such a world, given the world you and I live in? Who would dare set John's vision to such bold and beautiful music as Danner has? And who would dare to sing it?

So there are the days I cry at the anthem, and at the text it trumpets, because I wonder, as Buechner sometimes wonders, whether it can really be true, this business about God and the hope to which we have been called. The eyes of my heart sometimes seem to share my physical eyes' extreme nearsightedness, and I can't catch a glimpse of what John saw. There are the days I, unlike Naya, can't almost believe the words are (as the voice tells John they are) "trustworthy and true."

But on most days, I am somewhere in between. And I think I have learned that the truth of John's vision, like the truths Buechner shared with his mother in that letter he wrote to her, is a truth probably best not shouted—or, at least, shouted, or sung in epic style, only infrequently.

The voice John heard coming from the throne was loud, but that was because it was the voice of God. Sometimes, at least, when we hear a word from God, we, in our faltering human voices, would do better to repeat it softly. The vision of the Holy City is one of those truths best told delicately: a beautiful dream we believe will come true, but which loses much of its loveliness if shouted at the top of our lungs.

*God of the future, may our anticipation of the New Jerusalem's dazzling light never keep us from seeing the suffering of the world around us, and may the triumphant songs of praise we can already hear sounding from tomorrow never stop us from hearing cries of pain today that you call us to answer in the name and with the love of your Son, Jesus Christ. Amen.*

# Notes

## Session 1

1. M. Eugene Boring, "The Gospel of Matthew," *The New Interpreter's Bible*, Vol. VIII (Nashville: Abingdon Press, 1995), 453.
2. Craig S. Keener, *The IVP Bible Background Commentary: New Testament* (Downers Grove, IL: InterVarsity Press, 1993), 117.
3. Englishman's Greek Concordance, http://biblehub.com/greek /e_rgasato_2038.htm, accessed December 13, 2017.
4. The Free Dictionary, s.v. "Erg," http://www.thefreedictionary.com /Erg+(unit), accessed December 13, 2017.
5. R. Alan Culpepper, "The Gospel of Luke," *The New Interpreter's Bible*, Vol. IX (Nashville: Abingdon Press, 1995), 362.
6. Ron Wolfson, "How to Make a Shiva Call," My Jewish Learning, https://www.myjewishlearning.com/article/how-to-make-a-shiva -call/, accessed December 13, 2017.
7. Ibid.
8. J. Clinton McCann Jr., "The Book of Psalms," *The New Interpreter's Bible*, Vol. IV (Nashville: Abingdon Press, 1996), 1176.

## Session 2

1. Croesus was a sixth-century BC Greek king famed for his wealth. https://www.britannica.com/biography/Croesus, accessed December 13, 2017.

2. W. Sibley Towner, "The Book of Ecclesiastes," *The New Interpreter's Bible*, Vol. V (Nashville: Abingdon Press, 1997), 279.
3. Frederick Buechner, *The Sacred Journey* (1982; New York: HarperSanFrancisco, 1996), 4.
4. Englishman's Greek Concordance, http://biblehub.com/greek/charakte_r_5481.htm, accessed December 13, 2017.
5. Online Etymology Dictionary, s.v. "Character," http://www.etymonline.com/word/character, accessed December 13, 2017.
6. Buechner, *Sacred Journey*, 77.
7. Frederick Buechner, "Quote of the Day," June 8, 2016, http://www.frederickbuechner.com/quote-of-the-day/2016/6/8/money, accessed December 13, 2017.

## Session 3

1. For more on James Merrill's life and work, see https://www.poetryfoundation.org/poets/james-merrill.
2. Frederick Buechner, *Godric* (San Francisco: HarperSanFrancisco, 1980), 37.
3. Leslie C. Allen, "The First and Second Books of Chronicles," *The New Interpreter's Bible*, Vol. III (Nashville: Abingdon Press, 1999), 299.
4. Online Etymology Dictionary, s.v. "Paradise," https://www.etymonline.com/word/paradise, accessed December 13, 2017.
5. The Church of England, "The Order for the Burial of the Dead," *Book of Common Prayer*, https://www.churchofengland.org/prayer-and-worship/worship-texts-and-resources/book-common-prayer/burial-dead, accessed December 13, 2017.

## Session 4

1. Pheme Perkins, "The Letter to the Ephesians," *The New Interpreter's Bible*, Vol. XI (Nashville: Abingdon Press, 2000), 381.
2. Englishman's Greek Concordance, http://biblehub.com/greek/dunameo_s_1411.htm, accessed December 13, 2017.
3. Buechner, *Sacred Journey*, 22.